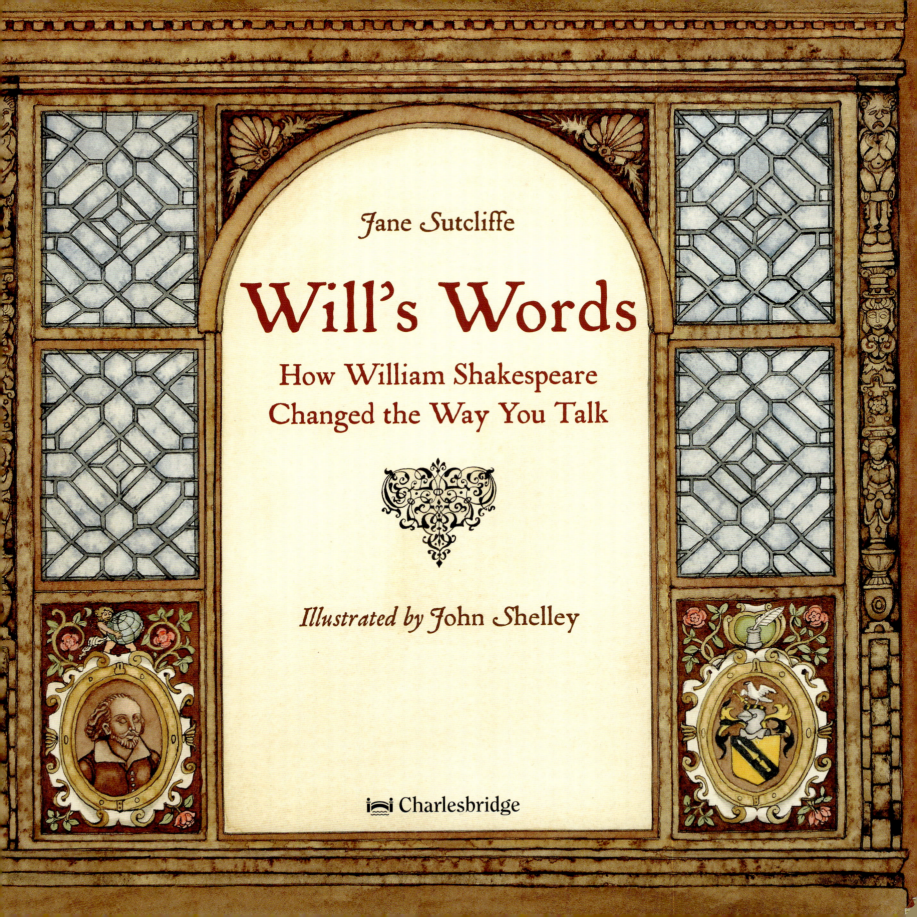

Jane Sutcliffe

Will's Words

How William Shakespeare
Changed the Way You Talk

Illustrated by John Shelley

Charlesbridge

Dear Reader:

We have to talk. I have failed you. I set out to write a book about the Globe Theatre and its great storyteller, William Shakespeare. About how the man was an absolute genius with words and wove those words into the most brilliant and moving plays ever written.

But that's just the trouble. You see, I wanted to tell you the story in my own words. But Will Shakespeare's words are there, too, popping up all over the place.

It's not my fault. Really. Will's words are everywhere. They're bumping into our words all the time, and we don't even know it. So how could I help it, **for goodness' sake**?

There, you see what I mean? Those are Will's words, all mixed in with mine. People just love his plays, and they've kept on loving them for hundreds of years—*hundreds*! And the more they love his plays, the more they use his words. Now his words and sayings are everywhere, ending up in the stuff we say and write every day. I couldn't avoid them if I tried—and I *did* try.

Well, I suppose **what's done is done**.

Oh. Right.

Maybe I'll just stop now and let you read the book.

Yours truly,
The Author

WILL'S WORDS: For goodness' sake

WHAT IT MEANS: When you look at these words, you can see that they really mean "for the sake of being good," and that's just what the saying meant in Will's time. Nowadays people use it more like "Doggone it."

WHERE IT COMES FROM: HENRY VIII, ACT 3, SCENE 1. *The bad guy in the play tells the queen she should change her behavior for the sake of goodness.*

WILL'S WORDS: What's done is done

WHAT IT MEANS: You can't change what you've done, so don't worry about it.

WHERE IT COMES FROM: MACBETH, ACT 3, SCENE 2. *Macbeth feels guilty after murdering the king. His wife tells him there's no use losing sleep over it since what's done is done. (Yeah, it wasn't a good excuse four hundred years ago, and it still isn't today.)*

In 1606 London was a bustling, jostling, clanging, singing, stinking, head-chopping, pickpocketing wonder of a city.

You would probably need a break from a city like that.

That's why London was also a play-going city. There was a play going on every day of the week except Sunday. Sometimes there were two or three.

When it came to plays, people in London thought you couldn't have **too much of a good thing**.

As many as eighteen thousand people a week made their way to the city's playhouses. That's nearly one in every ten Londoners. About the only thing that kept a London playgoer at home was an **outbreak** of the plague.

WILL'S WORDS: **Too much of a good thing**

WHAT IT MEANS: More of something good may be bad. (If you've ever eaten a whole bag of gummy worms at once, you already know what this means.)

WHERE IT COMES FROM: AS YOU LIKE IT, ACT 4, SCENE 1. *A woman teases her boyfriend that if one boyfriend is good, twenty must be even better. Or is that too much of a good thing?*

WILL'S WORD: **Outbreak**

WHAT IT MEANS: Will used this word to describe a sudden outburst of feeling. Nowadays it means the sudden start of something like an illness or a war.

WHERE IT COMES FROM: HAMLET, ACT 2, SCENE 1. *A nosy father wants to know what his hotheaded son is getting into. Will his friends tattle about his outbreaks of bad behavior?*

Good plays need good playwrights. And the most brilliant playwright in London was Mr. William Shakespeare. From butchers and bakers to lords and ladies, everyone looked forward to the **excitement** of a Will Shakespeare play.

WILL'S WORD: **Excitement**

WHAT IT MEANS: A feeling of "Bring it on!"
This was still a fairly new word in Will's time.
He helped people get excited about "excitement."

WHERE IT COMES FROM: HAMLET, ACT 4,
SCENE 4. *There's a lot of excitement in Hamlet's*
family. And not the good kind.

It all started with a waving flag. At about one o'clock in the afternoon, a banner was raised from the playhouse roof.

The flag signaled that the playhouse was now open. All **of a sudden**, London's streets were flooded with men, women, and children. Whole troops of them made their way across the Thames River by bridge or by boat to the fairest playhouse in the city, the Globe.

The Globe

WILL'S WORDS: **Of a sudden**

WHAT IT MEANS: Suddenly. We usually add an "all," as in "all of a sudden."

WHERE IT COMES FROM: THE TAMING OF THE SHREW, ACT I, SCENE I. *One character asks another if it's possible to fall in love suddenly.*

The Globe didn't look much like today's theaters. In fact, it looked something like a small, round football stadium with a thatched awning. It had three floors of seats around a big open space and a stage. It had vendors selling fruit, nuts, and beer. It had room for three thousand people. What it didn't have: any place for those people to go to the bathroom. Trying to find a restroom at the Globe would have been a **wild-goose chase**.

WILL'S WORDS: **Wild-goose chase**

WHAT IT MEANS: In Will's time a wild-goose chase was a horse race with riders following close behind a lead horse, like geese in flight. Now it means a useless search, like trying to catch a wild goose.

WHERE IT COMES FROM: ROMEO AND JULIET, ACT 2, SCENE 4. *Romeo's friend tells him that trying to follow his ideas is like a wild-goose chase. (Will used this saying only once. Trying to find it in another play would be a wild-goose chase.)*

Everyone dropped a penny in a ceramic pot called a "money box" to get in. (During the play the boxes were locked away in an office—the "box office.") Upper-class folk were lucky. They could pay a little more and sit. Poor people stood in the open yard, crammed in tight, with neighbor elbowing neighbor.

Of course, there were always those people who went just to show off their **fashionable** clothes. They paid extra to sit in the Lords' Rooms on the balcony just behind the stage. Everyone could see and admire them, but they ended up looking at the backs of the actors' heads. That might not seem like they were getting their **money's worth**, but they didn't mind.

WILL'S WORD: **Fashionable**

WHAT IT MEANS: In style. Like a lot of Will's words, this one was around already. But it's not a stretch to say that "fashionable" is still fashionable because of Shakespeare.

WHERE IT COMES FROM: *Will used this word in two plays.* In TIMON OF ATHENS, ACT 5, SCENE 1, *a character says that making promises is fashionable. Keeping them is another matter.*

WILL'S WORDS: **Money's worth**

WHAT IT MEANS: Value for what you spend. Entrance to the Globe cost the same as a loaf of bread. That's getting your money's worth.

WHERE IT COMES FROM: LOVE'S LABOUR'S LOST, ACT 2, SCENE 1. *A character wants what's owed him and demands his money's worth.*

Backstage, the actors got into their costumes. They were nearly ready.

A blast from a rooftop trumpet got any stragglers **hurrying**. Then everyone waited **with bated breath** for the play to begin.

The actors took the stage. Actors. Not actresses. London had a no-girls-allowed rule when it came to acting. Women's parts were played by boys in dresses—though some of them must have been **a sorry sight**.

WILL'S WORD: Hurry

WHAT IT MEANS: To go faster or to rush. How many times a day does someone tell you to hurry up? Blame Will. He helped make the word popular.

WHERE IT COMES FROM: THE COMEDY OF ERRORS, ACT 5, SCENE 1. *A character describes how her husband went crazy and hurried through the street.*

WILL'S WORDS: With bated breath

WHAT IT MEANS: In Will's time it meant with a hushed voice. Now it means holding your breath because you know something big is about to happen.

WHERE IT COMES FROM: THE MERCHANT OF VENICE, ACT 1, SCENE 3. *A character who's been mistreated asks if he's supposed to speak to the bully like a servant, with bated breath.*

WILL'S WORDS: A sorry sight

WHAT IT MEANS: Not looking so good.

WHERE IT COMES FROM: MACBETH, ACT 2, SCENE 2. *After killing the king, Macbeth says his bloody hands are a sorry sight.*

There was no hush when the play began.
Playgoers talked, crunched apples, cracked
nuts, guzzled beer, and belched to their
heart's content all through the play.
Sometimes they talked back to the actors.

London audiences weren't exactly known
for being **well behaved**.

WILL'S WORDS: Heart's content

WHAT IT MEANS: Will used this to mean "a happy heart." Now we use the phrase "to your heart's content" to mean "as much as you want."

WHERE IT COMES FROM: HENRY VI, PART 2, ACT 1, SCENE 1. *The king is in love and gives a speech about "the fulness of my heart's content."*

WILL'S WORDS: Well behaved

WHAT IT MEANS: Being good or polite.

WHERE IT COMES FROM: THE MERRY WIVES OF WINDSOR, ACT 2, SCENE 1. *A man who is not at all well behaved sends the same love letter to two women. Those merry wives will teach him a lesson.*

Being an actor, or "player," in a Shakespeare play was no easy job. A player might have to learn two, three, or four parts. And there were usually six *different* plays a week. Pity the poor fellow who forgot his lines. The audience would shout and pelt him with their snacks. Then the other players would **send him packing** quick enough.

WILL'S WORDS: **Send someone packing**

WHAT IT MEANS: To throw someone out. Will also gave us the phrase "good riddance," which is a handy thing to say when you send someone packing.

WHERE IT COMES FROM: HENRY IV, PART 1, ACT 2, SCENE 4. *A character threatens to throw out the king's messenger. He'll send the man packing!*

On some days the play was a comedy. These were lighthearted stories, often about mistaken identity or misplaced **love letters**. In *Twelfth Night* a female character dresses up as a male. That means a boy was playing a woman playing a boy. That sounds confusing, but it's all in good fun, and the play ends on a happy note with weddings for everybody. The playgoers **laughed themselves into stitches**.

WILL'S WORDS: **Love letter**

WHAT IT MEANS: A mushy note. There have always been love letters. You have to wonder: What did they call them before Will?

WHERE IT COMES FROM: TWO GENTLEMEN OF VERONA, ACT 3, SCENE 1. *There are lots of love letters flying back and forth here.*

WILL'S WORDS: **Laugh oneself into stitches**

WHAT IT MEANS: To laugh so hard you get a pain in your side. That Will must have been a fun guy if he knew that a good belly laugh can really hurt.

WHERE IT COMES FROM: TWELFTH NIGHT, ACT 3, SCENE 2. *Characters laugh themselves into stitches when a snooty fellow gets a joke played on him and ends up looking very silly.*

On other days the play was a tragedy, centered on some terrible **foul play**. In *Hamlet* a ghost reveals a dark secret. *Macbeth* has cackling witches, a murdered king, an evil couple, guilty nightmares, an imaginary dagger, and another ghost. Shakespeare's tragedies were shocking enough to **make people's hair stand on end**.

WILL'S WORDS: **Foul play**

WHAT IT MEANS: A dirty deed. Will gave us the phrase "fair play," too.

WHERE IT COMES FROM: HAMLET, ACT 1, SCENE 2. *Hamlet is told that the ghost of his dead father has been seen. Could the man's death have been foul play?*

WILL'S WORDS: **Make your hair stand on end**

WHAT IT MEANS: Give you a serious case of the creeps.

WHERE IT COMES FROM: HAMLET, ACT 1, SCENE 5. *A ghost tells a scary tale—but Will doesn't say the story is "scary." Instead he says it will freeze your blood, make your eyes bug out, and make your hair stick out like the quills on a porcupine. Way scarier!*

The history plays were always crowd favorites. These were stories about kings and queens from England's past. In *Henry V* a king sets off to war and becomes a great ruler, even though he does some pretty nasty things. In *Richard III* a **cold-blooded** tyrant will stop at nothing, even murder, to be crowned king.

Shakespeare's histories have noble heroes and scheming villains, battles and duels—and lots of characters who end up **dead as a doornail**. London playgoers loved watching their country's past come to life on the stage.

WILL'S WORD: Cold-blooded

WHAT IT MEANS: Unfeeling. Will also gave us these other "bloody" expressions: "hot-blooded" and "bloodstained."

WHERE IT COMES FROM: KING JOHN, ACT 3, SCENE 1. *A very angry woman calls a character a "cold-blooded slave."*

WILL'S WORDS: Dead as a doornail

WHAT IT MEANS: Dead. Really dead. This phrase was already old when Will used it, but without him it might well have ended up, um, dead as a doornail.

WHERE IT COMES FROM: HENRY VI, PART 2, ACT 4, SCENE 10. *A weak, starving character has some big talk for another man, saying he'll take him on—and five more men—and leave them all dead as a you-know-what.*

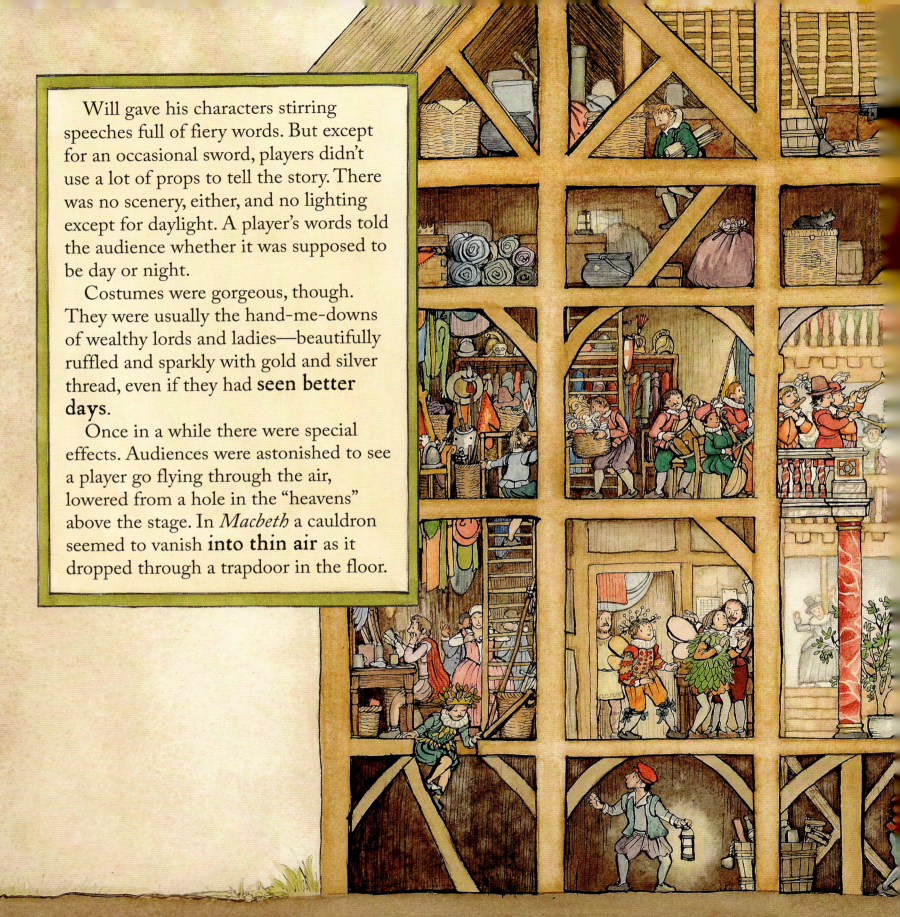

Will gave his characters stirring speeches full of fiery words. But except for an occasional sword, players didn't use a lot of props to tell the story. There was no scenery, either, and no lighting except for daylight. A player's words told the audience whether it was supposed to be day or night.

Costumes were gorgeous, though. They were usually the hand-me-downs of wealthy lords and ladies—beautifully ruffled and sparkly with gold and silver thread, even if they had **seen better days**.

Once in a while there were special effects. Audiences were astonished to see a player go flying through the air, lowered from a hole in the "heavens" above the stage. In *Macbeth* a cauldron seemed to vanish **into thin air** as it dropped through a trapdoor in the floor.

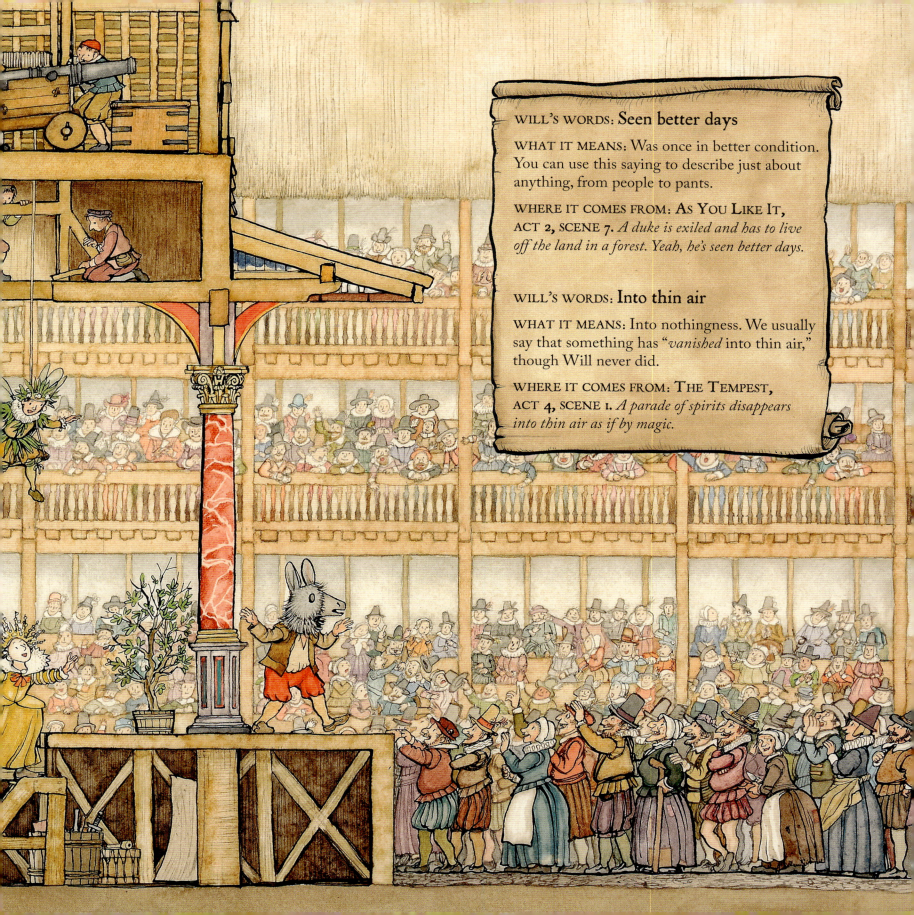

WILL'S WORDS: **Seen better days**

WHAT IT MEANS: Was once in better condition. You can use this saying to describe just about anything, from people to pants.

WHERE IT COMES FROM: AS YOU LIKE IT, ACT 2, SCENE 7. *A duke is exiled and has to live off the land in a forest. Yeah, he's seen better days.*

WILL'S WORDS: **Into thin air**

WHAT IT MEANS: Into nothingness. We usually say that something has "*vanished*" into thin air," though Will never did.

WHERE IT COMES FROM: THE TEMPEST, ACT 4, SCENE 1. *A parade of spirits disappears into thin air as if by magic.*

Most of Will's plays had no fancy extras, though. Usually it was just actors saying Will's words on a bare stage. For three hours, or four, or five, the audience sat or stood, often in rain or cold, listening in **amazement** to those glorious words. Because **the long and the short of it** was this: no one could tell a story like Mr. William Shakespeare.

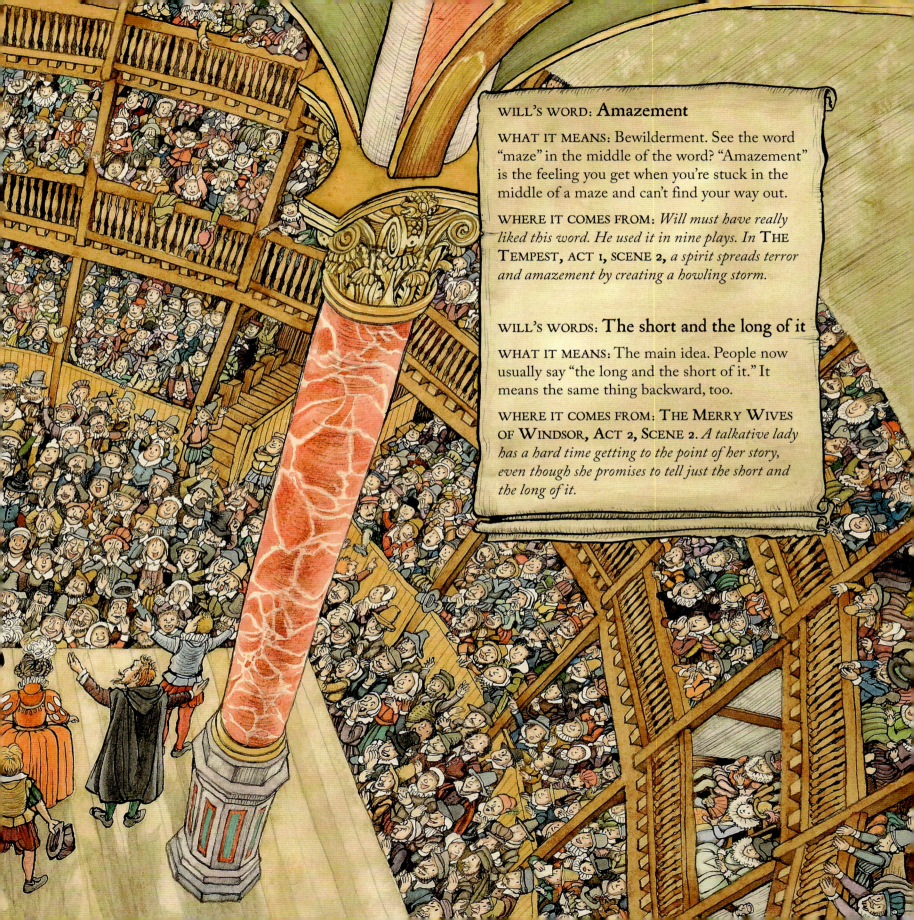

WILL'S WORD: **Amazement**

WHAT IT MEANS: Bewilderment. See the word "maze" in the middle of the word? "Amazement" is the feeling you get when you're stuck in the middle of a maze and can't find your way out.

WHERE IT COMES FROM: *Will must have really liked this word. He used it in nine plays. In* THE TEMPEST, ACT 1, SCENE 2, *a spirit spreads terror and amazement by creating a howling storm.*

WILL'S WORDS: **The short and the long of it**

WHAT IT MEANS: The main idea. People now usually say "the long and the short of it." It means the same thing backward, too.

WHERE IT COMES FROM: THE MERRY WIVES OF WINDSOR, ACT 2, SCENE 2. *A talkative lady has a hard time getting to the point of her story, even though she promises to tell just the short and the long of it.*

And when the audience went home, they took Will's words with them.

An apprentice didn't just complain that his master was stubborn. He said the man would **not budge an inch**.

A wife didn't just say that her husband's relatives were greedy. She grumbled that she was being **eaten out of house and home**.

Was a young man acting jealous? That was because he had been bitten by the **green-eyed monster**, his friends teased.

WILL'S WORDS: Not budge an inch

WHAT IT MEANS: Not move or change your mind even a little. We use this phrase exactly the same way Will did. It seems that stubborn people haven't changed much in four hundred years.

WHERE IT COMES FROM: THE TAMING OF THE SHREW, INDUCTION, SCENE 1. *A tavern keeper tells a drunken customer he has to pay for the glasses he's broken or she'll call the police. He says he won't, and he won't budge an inch.*

WILL'S WORDS: Eaten out of house and home

WHAT IT MEANS: Eaten everything you've got. Really, everything.

WHERE IT COMES FROM: HENRY IV, PART 2, ACT 2, SCENE 1. *A widow complains that a man has eaten her out of house and home. Her next line explains what she means: "He hath put all my substance into that fat belly of his."*

WILL'S WORDS: Green-eyed monster

WHAT IT MEANS: Jealousy. Four hundred years ago the color green was thought to be the color of jealousy. (That's why we say "green with envy.") Shakespeare just gave it eyes and attitude.

WHERE IT COMES FROM: OTHELLO, ACT 3, SCENE 3. *The villain tells the hero of the play to beware that green-eyed monster jealousy—then he does everything he can to make him jealous.*

In 1616 William Shakespeare died. A few years later his plays were collected and published in a book. People were able to go right on enjoying his plays year after year. Before long, Will's words were everywhere.

After a while a funny thing happened. The more people said all those words, the more they forgot that they were William Shakespeare's words. His words became part of what we say every day. After four hundred years, they still are.

Will's words have become—why, they have become **household words**.

WILL'S WORDS: **Household words**

WHAT IT MEANS: Stuff we say every day. The words "household words" are now household words. Does it get any cooler than that?

WHERE IT COMES FROM: HENRY V, ACT 4, SCENE 3. *The king rallies his troops for battle by telling them that everyone will remember their bravery and that their names will be as familiar as household words.*

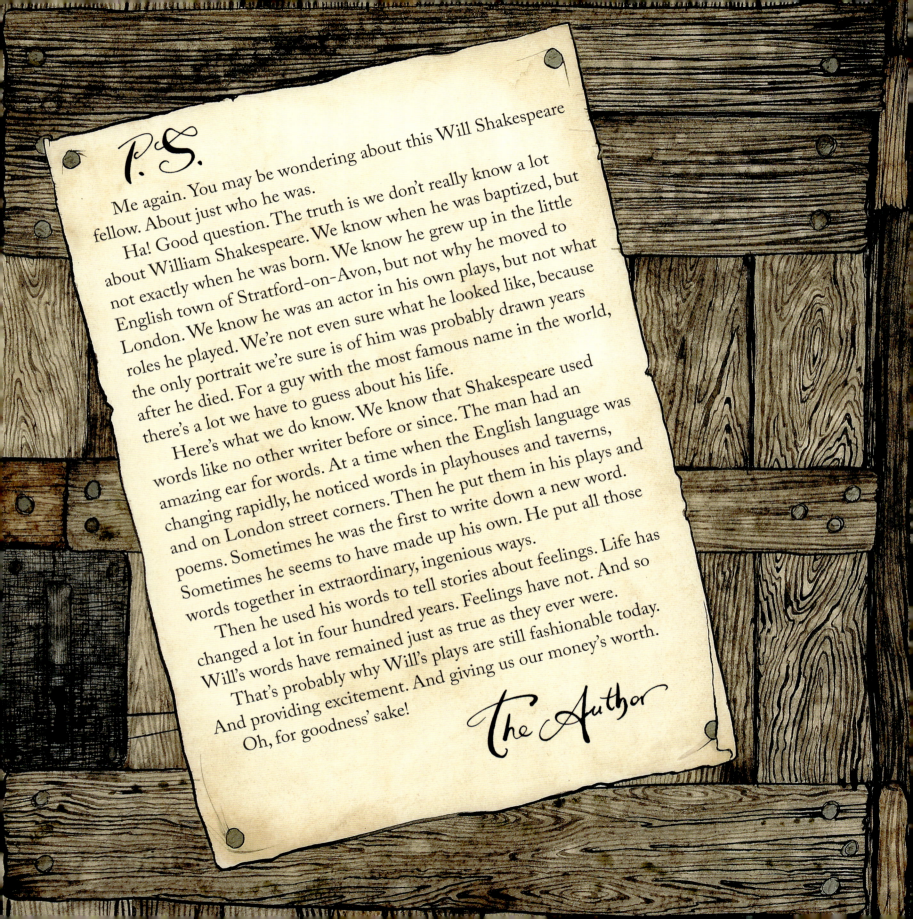

P.S.

Me again. You may be wondering about this Will Shakespeare fellow. About just who he was.

Ha! Good question. The truth is we don't really know a lot about William Shakespeare. We know when he was baptized, but not exactly when he was born. We know he grew up in the little English town of Stratford-on-Avon, but not why he moved to London. We know he was an actor in his own plays, but not what roles he played. We're not even sure what he looked like, because the only portrait we're sure is of him was probably drawn years after he died. For a guy with the most famous name in the world, there's a lot we have to guess about his life.

Here's what we do know. We know that Shakespeare used words like no other writer before or since. The man had an amazing ear for words. At a time when the English language was changing rapidly, he noticed words in playhouses and taverns, and on London street corners. Then he put them in his plays and poems. Sometimes he was the first to write down a new word. Sometimes he seems to have made up his own. He put all those words together in extraordinary, ingenious ways.

Then he used his words to tell stories about feelings. Life has changed a lot in four hundred years. Feelings have not. And so Will's words have remained just as true as they ever were. That's probably why Will's plays are still fashionable today. And providing excitement. And giving us our money's worth. Oh, for goodness' sake!

The Author

Time Line

1564	William Shakespeare was christened April 26 in Stratford-on-Avon. We celebrate his birthday April 23.
1582	Will married Anne Hathaway.
1583	Their daughter Susanna was born.
1585	Their twins Judith and Hamnet were born.
1589–1594	Will's first plays, including *Henry VI* and *Richard III*, were produced.
1592–1593	Playhouses in London were closed because of the plague.
1594	The Lord Chamberlain's Men, an acting company, was formed. Shakespeare was both an actor and a playwright.
1594 or 1595	*Romeo and Juliet* was a huge hit.
1596	Hamnet Shakespeare died.
1599	The Globe Theatre was built. Will was part owner.
1599–1608	Will wrote his greatest plays, including *Hamlet*, *Twelfth Night*, and *Macbeth*.
1603	Queen Elizabeth I died; James I became king. The Lord Chamberlain's Men became the King's Men.
1603–1604	Playhouses in London were closed again because of the plague.
1607–1613	Will completed the last plays that he wrote without a collaborator, including *The Tempest*.
1611?	Will returned to Stratford-on-Avon.
1612 or 1613	Will collaborated with another writer on his final plays, including *Henry VIII*.
1613	The Globe burned to the ground during the first performance of *Henry VIII*.
1614	The rebuilt Globe opened.
1616	William Shakespeare died April 23.
1623	His friends published a collection of his plays, now known as the First Folio.
1997	The modern Globe opened in London.

Bibliography

Ackroyd, Peter. *Shakespeare: The Biography.* New York: Anchor Books, 2010. Kindle edition.

Bryson, Bill. *The Mother Tongue: English & How It Got That Way.* New York: Avon Books, 1990.

Bryson, Bill. *Shakespeare: The World as Stage.* Eminent Lives. New York: HarperCollins, 2009. Kindle edition.

Dyer, Daniel. *All the World's a Stage: The Worlds of William Shakespeare.* Amazon Digital Services, 2012. Kindle edition.

Epstein, Norrie. *The Friendly Shakespeare: A Thoroughly Painless Guide to the Best of the Bard.* New York: Penguin Books, 1993.

Ganeri, Anita. *What They Don't Tell You About Shakespeare.* London: Hodder Children's Books, 1996.

Greenblatt, Stephen. *Will in the World: How Shakespeare Became Shakespeare.* New York: W. W. Norton, 2004.

Gurr, Andrew. *Playgoing in Shakespeare's London.* New York: Cambridge University Press, 2004.

Gurr, Andrew. *The Shakespearean Stage 1574–1642.* New York: Cambridge University Press, 2009.

Kaiser, Scott. *Shakespeare's Wordcraft.* New York: Limelight Editions, 2007.

Langley, Andrew. *Shakespeare's Theatre.* New York: Oxford University Press, 1999.

Martin, Gary. "135 Phrases Coined by William Shakespeare." *Phrase Finder.* Accessed October 2, 2013. www.phrases.org.uk/meanings/phrases-sayings-shakespeare.html.

McQuain, Jeffrey, and Stanley Malless. *Coined by Shakespeare: Words and Meanings First Penned by the Bard.* Springfield, MA: Merriam-Webster, 1998.

Porter, Stephen. *Shakespeare's London: Everyday Life in London 1580–1616.* Gloucestershire, UK: Amberley, 2011.

"Shakespeare Quotes." *eNotes.* Accessed October 24, 2013. www.enotes.com/shakespeare-quotes/index.

Shakespeare, William. *William Shakespeare Ultimate Collection.* Edited by Darryl Marks. Houston: Everlasting Flames, 2010. Kindle edition.

Stanley, Diane, and Peter Vennema. *Bard of Avon: The Story of William Shakespeare.* New York: Mulberry Books, 1998.

Thomson, Peter. *Shakespeare's Theatre.* New York: Routledge, 1992.

For John William and Amanda—J. Sutcliffe
The illustrations are for my father, Ken—J. Shelley

Special thanks to Angus Fletcher, associate professor of English
and film studies at the Ohio State University, for his invaluable
expertise and advice.

Published by Charlesbridge
85 Main Street
Watertown, MA 02472
(617) 926-0329
www.charlesbridge.com

Library of Congress Cataloging-in-Publication Data
Sutcliffe, Jane, author.
Will's words: how William Shakespeare changed the way you talk/Jane Sutcliffe;
illustrated by John Shelley.
pages cm
ISBN 978-1-58089-638-2 (reinforced for library use)
ISBN 978-1-60734-855-9 (ebook)
ISBN 978-1-60734-856-6 (ebook pdf)
1. Shakespeare, William, 1564–1616—Language. 2. English language—
Early modern, 1500–1700—Terms and phrases. I. Shelley, John, 1959– illustrator. II. Title.
PR3077.S88 2015
822.3'3—dc23   2014049187

Printed in China
(hc) 10 9 8 7 6 5 4 3 2 1

Illustrations done in pen and ink on Fabriano hot-press paper and painted in watercolor
Display type set in P22 Mayflower
Text type set in Adobe Caslon
Color separations by Colourscan Print Co Pte Ltd, Singapore
Printed by 1010 Printing International Limited in Huizhou, Guangdong, China
Production supervision by Brian G. Walker
Designed by Susan Mallory Sherman